The Approaching Promise

Molana Salaheddin Ali Nader Shah ibn
Molana-al-Moazam Hazrat
Shah Maghsoud Sadegh Angha "Pir Oveyssi"

School of Islamic Sufism
Maktab Tarighat Oveyssi Shahmaghsoudi®

Shahmaghsoudi (Angha) Heritage Series on Sufism

Library of Congress Cataloging-in-Publication Data

Salaheddin Ali Nader Shah Angha, 1942–
[Muqtarib. Polyglot]
The approaching promise / Salaheddin Ali Nader Shah ibn Molana-al
-Moazam Hazrat Shah Maghsoud Sadegh Angha.
p.   cm. — (Shahmaghsoudi (Angha) heritage series on Sufism)
Includes original Persian text with English, Arabic, French, Italian translation.
1. Maktab Tarighe Oveyssi Shahmaghsoudi—Prayer books and
devotions—English. I. Title. II. Series.
BP189.7.M28S2512   1989
297'.43—dc19   89–5585 CIP

ISBN 0–8191–7403–3 (pbk.: alk. paper)

Contents

About the Author

The Approaching Promise is one of several recent works by Hazrat Pir, Molana Salaheddin Ali Nader Shah ibn Molana-al-Moazam Hazrat Shah Maghsoud Sadegh Angha. He is the forty-second Master of the School of Islamic Sufism, the Maktab Tarighat Oveyssi Shahmaghsoudi. His father, grandfather, and great-grandfather were also Masters of the School, in the line of Teachers extending back 1,400 years to the Prophet Mohammad (peace be upon him).

Recently, Hazrat Pir was asked if the Masterhood of the Oveyssi School always passed from father to son. He replied that his father had once said to him that he was just like any of the other students in the School of Islamic Sufism, all of whom receive the same education. The result of the education may differ, however; elevation and graduation depend upon purity, love, devotion, truthfulness, and obedience. However, Hazrat Pir emphasized that the results he had obtained during the course of his training were verified and approved by his father, the Master, who then granted him the Masterhood.

Hazrat Pir first received his holy and spiritual instructions from his grandfather, Molana Hazrat Mir Ghotbeddin Mohammad Angha, Pir Oveyssi. Then, when he showed special capacities, his father began further instructions. Hazrat Pir, born into this great teaching and into these circumstances, was thus prepared for the Masterhood of the Oveyssi School. Today, as Master, Hazrat Pir is the holder of the cloak of Abraham (peace be upon him) and Mohammad himself (peace be upon him).

Under his direction centers around the world serve more than 300,000 people with the Sufi teachings of the Oveyssi

School. In addition, he maintains homes for the aged and is himself directly involved in caring for those with acquired immune deficiency syndrome (AIDS).

May these teachings remove the imaginary, geographic, and traditional boundaries between West and East — for the Sun always rises from the East, the heart of the perfect Super Man.

Foreword

In reading *The Approaching Promise* by Molana Salaheddin Ali Nader Shah ibn Molana-al-Moazam Hazrat Shah Maghsoud Sadegh Angha, the forty-second Pir (Eminent Master) of the Maktab Tarighat Oveyssi Shahmaghsoudi, we are aware of the eminence of its author. The poem is a vessel of spiritual and religious thought for which I have not been formally prepared; yet it is that of a poet as well as a prophet, and so something can belong to all of us who live by a love and interest in language. We are invited in. Poetry is the property of those who can realize it, and it is in this light that we approach the words of a distinguished Sufi Master. Poetic thought shows us the mind and soul of the seer. . . . Poetic language reveals the hand of the sayer. With this entitlement we enter the text to experience the force field of the writer's reality in hopes of describing what is found.

The preamble to *The Approaching Promise* holds the statement that its four elements are written in terms of "the axis of Four, Five, Seven, Nine, and Six." We are told that the document was a revelation to Hazrat Pir. For those of us who have followed his recent literature, we are familiar with his work as divine revelation and its subsequent commitment to the page. The fact that *The Approaching Promise* flows in lines of specific length and number is perhaps not necessary knowledge for the reader, but it is of more than slight interest to the writers among us. Those of us who try to harness the moving word will marvel at lines that fall into specific mathematical patterns. To attempt such symmetry and to consciously arrange it is beyond that which most writers can accomplish or are willing to do. Relative to this text, then, is the mystery in its arrangement of words and lines that assume a natural mathematical unity, and finally we accept this more as inspiration than craft.

The text is a blueprint in which the forces — water, wind, earth, fire — are our guides. Each section can be described as a prayer, a chant, a prophesy. There is an infinite question posed after each section. The questions asked by Hazrat Pir are simply, "What happened to That? What became of It?" This reiteration occurs at the end of each of the four sections. By posing these questions Hazrat Pir asks us to evaluate what we have, what we have lost, what we have not used, what we have foregone. He brings us this message — our given treasure — with subtle, penetrating kindness. We notice in the first reading that each of the four stanzas are in eleven lines, and each begins with the word That. Through the use of fire, wind, water, and earth, the writer speaks to us of the journey of light — our existence beyond the elements of fire, wind, water and earth which are the basis for the physical forms of beings.

In his words, Hazrat Pir gives us the sun of knowledge. He describes it as "a radiant magnificent star ... that descends and penetrates." Through his eyes, we perceive particles of light drifting from the dust of the heavens. A brilliance of thought is inflamed by such dramatic phrases as "feverish hearts," "breath of life," "frenzy of love," "shooting star." These phrases also create a motion within the stanza. The first stanza, then, sets the tone for the whole. Its content creates the crystal of the poet's seeing: a mirror connecting all life and experience ... moving, moving through eternity like a star "descending and penetrating." In the subsequent lines of the first three stanzas we are given a listing of the exquisiteness of our existence — "that lustrous gleaming pearl," "that water drop," "the fields of endearing madness," "that entrusted jewel" — which we come to know is our essence and the heart's crystal we are born to carry. We are told of our perfection ... the promise of perfection ... and how we can be alive with its lustre. It is a poet we read. Hazrat Pir's words bring us close into the radiance of vision. We can understand interpretively the truth seen through his eyes. There is no way we can imagine the exact transference from the Persian language, but the imagery in this translation speaks for the probable beauty of the original.

The fourth section describes how we have castigated our gift. The words now are strong: dust, carcass, cesspool, mud. The language is stark in contrast to the previous stanzas that shimmer with the flowers and fruit of the poet's mind. The song turns harsh as children of the earth are described as "children of greed." The dust of the heavens descends to become "a swampland," and we are among those destined to die with our secret unrealized: "How can I not divulge, this was the treasure that was interred." The living treasure described by the poet dies with us. The poet's final cry is movement back from pain to freedom, however resigned: "Though I am enclosed in the coercion of time, yet the resplendent flame of this lantern I am." So ends the text.

The writing moves from an unenclosed, unlimited gift of glory through a bitter prophesy, leaving us with questions. Earthly confusions make us mistake our clumsy motions for flight. The message throughout is of the danger of such confusion. Will we die of spiritual hunger craving the illusion of food? It points out that the nourishment is in all time within us. But "What happened to That" — the work points again to our potential wreckage. The poem speaks of this world with a voice some of us may not hear. But through the poetry of its cry, the reader can appreciate and understand the promise of liberation and the dangers of captivity. Caught within the strivings of the world, we are told not to mistake activity for spiritual motion. The poem's structure is in five parts. It gains momentum through its listings and phraseology, and most especially through the repetition of a single word framing each line. It asks, at the end of each stanza of eleven lines, Where did all this go? The song ascends in three parts, becomes a dissonant cry in part four, and resolves itself back to song and a personal plea at its ending.

What is there for us to carry away from this small document? For the reader, there is a canon of thought, which is visually extraordinary, as well as an understanding of poetry and its cultural sources. There is — for those interested in the method by which experience is converted to poetry — the ecstasy of the singer and the enchantment of the song. In the poem's content there is the warning of quicksand and the choice given for immortality. This poem is a small symphony to all the senses. As modern individuals, if we take one message from its content, it may be a simple one — that unenlightened worldly activity will lose the soul. This prayer in five parts streams toward silence and takes us with it toward wonder. For those of us receptive to the visionary poem, it is a box of jewels. For those who wish serenity through poetry, reading it may be a beginning.

Grace Cavalieri
September 30, 1988
Washington, D.C.

Grace Cavalieri is a teacher and poet. She is the author of five books of poetry and eighteen plays, which have been produced throughout the country for stage and radio. Her career covers almost every aspect of teaching writing and broadcasting. After setting up a writing program for Antioch College, she became associate director in programming for the Public Broadcasting Service. She was senior program officer in media for the National Endowment for the Humanities and is host/producer of the only ongoing poetry program in the nation now in its twelfth year of broadcast. "The Poet and the Poem" is produced on WPFW-FM in Washington, D.C., and is distributed nationally to public radio stations.

Introduction

In reading *The Approaching Promise,* it is essential to consider the entire matter of Sufi writing and poetry as it has reached the West. The West here encompasses all the cultures for which this and other writings are translated from the original Persian and includes those speaking English, French, Arabic, and Italian.

Many books have been written over the years on the subject of Sufis and Sufism. Nearly all include translations of Sufi writing. Some of these are authored by Sufis and Sufi Masters, others by those known as orientalists.

The works written by Sufis and Sufi Masters most frequently come to the Western world in the form of poetry. Discourses and teachings are more rarely translated, although in recent years many more have become available.

For the Western world, the translation of Sufi writings is fortunate, because it makes the Sufi expression of union with God accessible to us. But as we read these translations, we must keep in mind that Persian is a complex and subtle language, full of nuances, meanings, and metaphors that lose some of their richness when translated. This is true no matter how careful the translation, how great the integrity of the translator. In addition, in different cultures things and experiences are viewed and expressed differently. For example, if we are expecting tomorrow to be a hot day, in English we say, "Tomorrow it will be hot." In Persian, however, we say, "Tomorrow the air will be hot." The English expression carries no reference to air at all, yet both experiences of temperature are approximately the same.

We can be sure that the translations by Sufis from the original Persian into English express as accurately as possible the content — the meanings, metaphors, and nuances — of the writings. But translations by those known as orientalists must be read with discrimination because we have no way of knowing the motivations, understandings, or philosophical perspectives held by the translators.

Among translations and writings by orientalists of this century are those of Arthur J. Arberry and Reynold A. Nicholson. Both these authors approach the subject of Sufism from a philosophical or academic viewpoint. For example, in *The Mystics of Islam: An Introduction to Sufism* (originally published in 1914 and reprinted many times, most recently in 1975), Nicholson describes the path of Sufism, its stages, its Saints, and the Unitive State. Arberry's work includes *The Doctrine of the Sufis,* first published in 1935. It is a translation of the *Kitāb al-Ta'arruf li-madhhab ahl al-taṣawwuf* of Kalabadhi, a Persian manuscript written in the tenth century A.D. and one of the earliest extant writings to reconcile Sufism and orthodox Islam. Another well-known translation is Edward Fitzgerald's rendition of the Rubaiyat of Omar Khayyam.

In these and other writings, Arberry, Nicholson, and Fitzgerald tend, as academics, to reference the subject of Sufism from a historical perspective. They are recounting their own perceptions of Sufi writings, and are not Sufis. Thus readers should not assume that their words represent the Truth of Sufism, for Sufism cannot be viewed from a historical or academic perspective, although Sufism has been present throughout much of recent recorded history. The Holy Prophets did not discover the Truth through academic pursuits. Sufism, moreover, is not a philosophy or way of thinking. It is rather the daily evolvement of the human being, a matter of experience and practice, a Knowledge applicable now. As Hazrat Pir, Molana Salaheddin Ali Nader Shah Angha says, *"Sufism is a reality of religion."* It is the cognition of the absolute Reality of Existence.

To illustrate, the combination of two parts hydrogen with one part oxygen (H_2O) always, everywhere on earth, produces water. If there exists one place on earth where this combination of hydrogen and oxygen does not produce water, then the formula does not express the absolute underlying truth of water and represents a manifestation rather than a law. A law can be described as something to which there is no exception; if one exception exists, then that law is destabilized and is no law at all. So it is with Sufism: it is always stable and founded on the unchanging, stable Truth which we must experience directly. Therefore, it is applicable.

Thousands of years ago, people had water to quench thirst. Today water still quenches thirst. It is always applicable. There has been no time in history when water could not be used to vanquish thirst. So it is that 5,000 years ago, the one who wanted Knowledge was driven by the same motivation to know. The Knowledge of Sufism is the same today as it was in that time and is implemented in the seeker today the same as then.

Nicholson describes at length similarities among Sufism, early Christianity, Gnosticism, Buddhism, and Greek philosophy or Neoplatonism. He asserts that Sufism was influenced greatly by these schools of thought, but he does not point out the element of duality that each of these teachings contains.

To understand this, consider the teachings of Christ and the language he uses. In the Bible, he speaks of the "Throne of God," the "Heavenly Kingdom" — in other words, of a state or a place. He describes and invites, and this is the highest level of his teachings. But such phrases as "His throne" and the "Right Hand of God" contain inherent duality. The matter of unity is deeper in Sufism than any other state.

Nicholson may see Sufism as a way of thought that takes these ideas as a starting point and builds upon them, but this is not so. Sufism was not influenced by thoughts and ideas from schools of thought, nor ideas from Christianity or Buddhism. To illustrate, in America a person would say, "I have a toothache," while in Japan a person would say, "I have a pain in my tooth." Other than the way the idea is expressed, what is the difference? Each experiences pain in the tooth and has the same reactions. The pain in one individual is not influenced by the pain in the other. The source is the individual's perceptions, and each individual experiences this reality. Thus, it can be seen that Nicholson is making a mistake when he states that Sufism has taken thoughts and ideas from other sources. In Sufism, we are instead describing something stable and unchangeable that does not have its roots in any mechanism of thought, something as stable and unchangeable as water that in all times and places has been the necessity of organisms and human beings for quenching thirst.

Clearly, then, we need to be careful not to make the mistake of thinking that reading an article or translation feeds our minds with a correct and true sense of the content and meaning of Sufism. The act of reading about Sufism is not the real thing. Sufism is rather a matter of learning and practicing by the teachings of the *Aref* (Sufi Master) himself.

Sufi poems and sayings are frequently quoted by Nicholson, Arberry, and others. Just as frequently they are explained by these authors in ways that are only sometimes accurate. In addition, most of the translations do not do full justice to the originals. A Sufi reading the same words sees an entirely different meaning in the same poems and passages. The Sufi discovers the inner Truth in each stage and announces that discovery in prose and poetry, which may seem to us as a new interpretation. Hazrat Pir, in his book *The Wealth of Solouk,* gives us a key to understanding the difference between the philosopher and the *Aref: "The philosopher wants to know, while the Aref knows."*

Each painter sees and paints a tree differently. The reality of the tree is the same; the tree does not change. The interpretation is different because it represents the sight, emotions, and inner feelings of each painter. But a Sufi discovers the Truth and puts it into the form of words and poems. The words may be different, but the words are explaining the One Truth. The state of discovering the Truth is the objective for the *Aref.*

In talking about the problems of translation, Hazrat Pir says about his recent work *The Secret Word,* "*My feelings are no longer in that English word, probably because the whole thing is there in Persian. If I had written in English maybe it would be there. Is a painting one who has painted? Now you are just describing. The painter is lost.*"

It is most important to know that the teachings in the School of Islamic Sufism have been passed from Master to Master for centuries. Each Master has passed the candle flame of Truth to the next, and with that flame each Master has lit — and continues to light — the candle flames of those who want to discover the Truth for themselves. If we take the candle flame as Truth, no place or time limits it. He is living among us, and we don't know Him because we have not sincerely wanted to.

For those who want to experience the depth of the real Knowledge, Sufism is not something old, not something covered with the dust and cobwebs of time. Nor can Sufism be represented as a system of beliefs, for belief to the Sufis is something entirely different than the belief as commonly held by people. Their belief springs from within as the result of following the teachings of the *Aref* to discover the Truth. For the Sufis, religion is not adherence to customs and ceremonies but something entirely different. Sufis adhere to the direct guidance of God. In this state of awareness, their religion is their Truth. And we see specifically in the Holy Koran that religion is the Truth. So the Sufis experience God's command-ments to reach the highest cognition and follow the Prophets' methods.

Sufis believe because their belief comes from knowing. When we have seen and experienced, then, and only then, can we truly believe. The Sufi's belief is a belief of knowing and cognition, not a belief rooted in tradition, bigotry, deduction, and reasoning.

Sufi writings, and Sufi poetry in particular, describe to the greatest extent possible the experience of the Sufi's union with God — the union with the Truth of Existence — and the Sufi's Love of God. At other times the Sufi poet is inspired by the pain of separation. Often the writings speak of the drunkenness caused by wine and may seem erotic in their metaphorical descriptions of ultimate love and union.

Love is often misunderstood, often confused with infatuations, likings, tendencies, and chance meetings, as a result of a need to vanquish some thirst for the temporary and temporal. Here is what Hazrat Pir says regarding Love: *"The source of whatever does happen in Existence is Love. Love does explain or translate at certain different levels. There is a love between two individuals; there is a love between the father and the mother and the child, and so forth. And there is also the love or the feeling of one individual with respect to the Creator. And also there is a Love which is the state of annihilation. In other words, physically you exist, but what does actually exist is the Existence which presents or translates through your physical being."* Love is only equal to Love. There is no relation, only a Giver. It is not a two-sided behavior.

Such an experience of union defies description in ordinary words; and those who have not had this experience are unable to understand the poetic expression of this union. When we read Sufi poetry, we should remember that the feelings evoked in us are not the reality of the words expressed by its authors. What do the words say? What feelings do they evoke? What questions do they engender? Molana-al-Moazam Hazrat Shah Maghsoud Sadegh Angha, Pir Oveyssi says in his book *The Mystery of Humanity,* "Words do not contain their meaning." Words can only be used to describe.

The mind receives signals and symbols as words and attempts to capture meaning through the mechanism of some matrix of information already stored or learned. If someone says to us, "I am good," we compare our "I" to what we think about that person's "I," our "good" to that person's "good." For example, that person's "good" may mean very healthy and happy; but if we have just recovered from a serious illness, we are likely to define "good" as meaning recovery from illness.

Hearing creates an understanding based upon a relation between two points, or persons, which exists in the mind of the one hearing. In other words, the mind's logical constructs listen and say, "This particular 'A' sounds like this certain 'B' that I already know or have some opinion about. Therefore, 'A' is equal to 'B'." For the Sufi, either there is no 'A' in the mind equal to any 'B', or there is a 100 percent difference.

We use certain words as symbols for things that each person holds in common experience, and this facilitates the communication of ideas. If 'A' says "tree," 'B' will understand the form as well as something about the structure and shape of the tree.

Other words, however, possess inherent dangers because there is no common experience of them upon which to build understanding. For example, for the words "Heaven," "Hell," "Paradise," or "God," there is no foundation for conveying any meaning because there is no direct, common experience. Using such words in conversation often pits concept against concept, one philosophical viewpoint against another philosophical viewpoint.

The equating mechanism of the mind satisfies itself with an explanation, while the truth of the matter remains obscured. But even the use of words that do have a base in common understanding cannot be said to convey meaning. They convey the symbol, not the thing represented. The word "candy" is understood symbolically but conveys no sweetness to the mouth. When heard, it may evoke such reactions as wanting the candy, or not wanting it; but it does not provide sweetness.

The brain, which is part of our body and mind system, has been given a place of importance far beyond its rightful place. It is instead a tool, a part of the system, much like a computer. If the brain were actually infallible in its ability to reason and make decisions, the current crisis of morality and ethics manifest in our societies would not exist.

Here are some of the words and teachings of Hazrat Pir, regarding the purpose and function of the brain:

If we don't realize what each system does, or what each should do, we don't organize and program it the way we should do. Let's make an example between the brain and a computer system. We give in all the information and then we push a few keys when we want certain information from it. That is how the brain works. But remember this: If the computer itself does not stay at a stable temperature and a stable frequency of electricity, it does not give us the proper answer. Or if you push the wrong key you get the wrong answer. The brain is the same way. It's a memory cell with all the information through the period of this life plus what you have inherited from the generations before you. If you push the wrong key, naturally you get the wrong answer.

In reading *The Approaching Promise*, it is important that we refrain from pressing the wrong buttons if we are to gain some understanding and insight into the words.

Consider an example from the world of science as representative of the dilemma posed by an experience of knowing that takes an instant to realize, longer to describe, and much longer to be understood by the scientific community and the world at large. Albert Einstein, father of the theory of general relativity, is said to have come upon his moment of knowing by pondering a simple question: How would a light wave look if you could run fast enough to catch up with it? Out of that instantly realized experience came mathematics so elaborate that it took several years to devise a test for even part of Einstein's theory. Note that only Einstein had the experience of realization directly, physically, and mentally, that only

Einstein harmonized at the level where he was able to experience that reality. Those who worked to prove his theory had a different experience — the experience of proving through experimentation.

Einstein was the discoverer because he was in a state to make the discovery. What he discovered was not new for him, however, but was rather something in existence that was already a part of his state. Others had to follow his theory, his formula for discovery, in order to experience it. So it can be said that he was the founder of a path. Had he not paved the road, no one could have experienced it.

Those who work to prove the theory experience Einstein's world, not their own. They know because of him. If he had not opened this knowledge to them, they would not know. Einstein's relation to a specific level of knowledge opened a new dimension, changed the nucleus of geometry to include space, time, and surface.

Einstein wanted to discover and find one unique Reality of Existence; but his great theory is rooted in the world of duality. He considered two points on a finite continuum as he was looking for a unity, with matter at one end and energy at the other.

The Truth of Existence in Sufism exists at the point of the Infinite, or Unification. To follow this example, it can be said that at the point where Unification exists, there is no matter or energy, thus the roots of Einstein's theory lie in duality. This topic is expounded in detail in Molana-al-Moazam Hazrat Shah Maghsoud's book *The Hidden Angles of Life*.

A seeker *(salek)*, through the guidance of the Master and his grace, is led to a personal experience of the Truth of Existence, the Infinite. There is no language by which this direct experience can be imparted. The transmission is instead made through a special language that is revealed only through the heart — through, for example, a language of the nerves that transfers impulses and sensations.

The language of words is a language of symbols, with each word symbolizing an object. We have the object, and we agree to establish a symbol in the form of a word. This works well enough when we are familiar with the source of what is represented. If we say "date," we are familiar with the fruit represented by the word. However, when we say "God," there is no common understanding or agreement about what is represented by the symbol. Representing the unknown by the symbol is often useless and leads to confusion. This does not mean, however, that reading about the Sufi path is pointless, or that achieving the goal of experiencing the Truth of Existence is beyond reach.

Sufi poetry and writing often express the experience of Union. One such expression is the following poem of Baba Kuhi Shirazi, a *salek* of the eleventh century A.D. An individual who has not experienced union with the Truth — found God — is unable to know the meaning of this state as expressed here; but an individual can take some of the elements of the poem as a guide in searching for a teacher who can lead him or her to this goal — union with God.

In the market, in the cloister — only God I saw.
In the valley and on the mountain — only God I saw.
Him have I seen beside me oft in tribulation;
In favour and in fortune — only God I saw.
In prayer and fasting, in praise and contemplation,
In the religion of the Prophet — only God I saw.
Neither soul nor body, accident nor substance,
Qualities nor causes — only God I saw.
I opened mine eyes and by the light of His face
    around me
In all the eye discovered — only God I saw.
Like a candle I was melting in His fire:
Amidst the flames out flashing — only God I saw.
Myself with mine own eyes I saw most clearly,
But when I looked with God's eyes — only God I saw.

I passed away into nothingness, I vanished,
And lo, I was the All-living — only God I saw.

Certainly, the poet presents to us here the idea that when we lose the illusionary individuation of self, the Universal Self is found. If we consider this illusionary self as a tiny drop of water that is led to the ocean and there joins with it, there is no drop, only ocean. However, nothing is lost in this Existence; the drop simply loses its imaginary boundaries in the Union with the ocean. In speaking about Sufi poetry, Hazrat Pir explains that *"In poetry or any other types of works, the person who is acting in it has to be in a certain state of feelings. He is trying to describe and present his feeling through the source of different items, like a painter. We all have seen brushes and paint, but there is a painter and there is a painter. One just paints, one is presenting himself through the paint, colors, and so forth. So is the poetry."*

On this earth, our bodies and cells are held together by pressures and gravities. The body is suitable for these specific circumstances. If we were to travel to the moon and had no suitable protection, the circumstances would not be suitable and the body could not exist. In the spiritual realm, the layers and the cells are more tender; they are formed under specific circumstances by the Spiritual Guide.

The road is open to all, but we don't know how to find it. The way is blocked by the limited contentment with traditional, unrelated ideas. The way to discover the path is shown in the lives of Moses, Jesus, and Mohammad (peace be upon them). They are the discoverers, and they endeavored to disclose the optimum Truth forever. Thus all seekers *(salekan)* follow, step-by-step, the instructions given by the Spiritual Guide of their time, in order to discover through the heart what their Guide has already discovered and knows.

But to compare ourselves to the example of Moses, Jesus, and Mohammad (peace be upon them) is to continue in duality. We can read their words, and the interpretations of other writers, in the Bible and Koran, but reading will not show us the way. The Bible and Koran are like road maps for unknown lands where the road signs are in a language we cannot understand by conventional means. The question, then, is, What are we going to do? How will we find the One who will show us the way?

On the subject of duality, Jalaleddin Rumi in the *Divan Shams Tabriz*, in dedication to his Master in the thirteenth century A.D., expresses Unity in these words:

> I have put duality away, I have seen that the two
>   worlds are one;
> One I seek, One I know, One I see, One I call.
> I am intoxicated with Love's cup, the two worlds have
>   passed out of my ken;
> I have no business save carouse and revelry.

Does Jalaleddin Rumi in the last line of this poem mean that he can now conduct his affairs in some flippant or irresponsible way? On the contrary. He means something entirely different. If we look up the words "carouse" and "revelry" in a standard thesaurus, the last line can be taken to mean "I have no business save vigorous, vital, celebration."

Here are similar words concerning the state of annihilation from Molana-al-Moazam Hazrat Shah Maghsoud Sadegh Angha, Pir Oveyssi, from his book *Message from the Soul:*

> Weariness and fatigue are alien to the state of my heart, but they will vanish if You fill my heart with Your grace. The foundation of my body is shaking from lack of energy, and the vision of my eyes is gradually turning dark, and if deprived of the light of seeing You, I will wither in pain.
>
> If in justice You choose to judge me by my deeds, it will be what my heart desires, and if in Your kindness You forgive my distressed soul, it will be Your mercy. All my deeds and intentions are for You. I am neither

aware of what I do nor have I any knowledge of the path I have tread or will follow.

My capital is poverty and the gift of the poor to Your divine presence is unworthy. O Forgiving One, do not leave me unto myself, but guide me to the glory within, and touch me with Your supreme kindness.

O Eternity! How great and precious You are.

The poet received the words himself from Existence, and Existence can again convey their meaning. As we read the words — and read them again with full contemplation and care to the words themselves — the Existence and spirituality of the poet lead our hearts and minds to a desire for awakening. If we want to see the sun that has risen from the East yesterday, we must open our eyes early in the morning to the sun today. And we will be released from darkness.

In describing and explaining Sufism, Hazrat Pir says, *"For some reason we have a tendency to separate and divide things, not only Sufism. But as Sufism exists in most societies it actually does not present and provide what Sufism might be, just so many ceremonies and things picked up from different groups. Sufism is a reality of religion, a state of awareness and cognition."*

"In Sufism," Hazrat Pir tells us, *"we are talking about the absolute, the essence which has no boundary anywhere."* If we consider the absolute essence as light (or a source of light) shining through a prism, it reveals different colors as components of the light, such as green, red, and purple. These can be thought of as the layers or levels of existence. Is the green, for example, the only light? Can it be differentiated from the light that is the source on the other side of the prism? It is not and it cannot because it is from and part of that source. To see this for ourselves, we can place a prism at the other end of the colors and observe how they once again become the same light as that from the original source. Between the prisms are the levels and layers of existence of life, but the source is one and the same light.

There is a source of life that presents itself continuously. What happened to it? Where did it go? This is the subject of *The Approaching Promise*. The poem places everything in the hands and will of God and then describes both metaphorically and figuratively the true condition of the Essence of Life, the evolution from this true condition of Existence into ordinary life, and the conditions of things to their final state. An acknowledgment of God's guidance and inspiration gives way in the final lines to a plea to God to be set free to fly from these dungeon walls.

* * *

I was in a very dark place without light. I groped in all directions looking for candle and matches. All of my thinking and reasoning could not show me the place where, in this darkness, these vital things were stored.

I wandered here and there, like dust in the winds; like a separated leaf from the Tree of Life, moving only by motivations, thought, and waves, aimlessly here and there.

I was like the temporary waves among all the waves on the Sea of Existence; like a bird without a nest, threatened, frightened, and homeless.

I was like a dog in the hands of the children of nature; they played with me in any way they desired.

I was like a tool for those who wanted to use me for their objectives; like a bare and wild land, uncultivated or paved.

This was my story before meeting Him.

For many years I had been searching for the Truth of my own existence. I read many books, listened to many people, and attended many meetings and groups. Only in the Sufi writings did I find any grain of what I thought I was seeking. Through these readings I collected many intellectual concepts about the subject matter. In personal meetings with those calling themselves Sufis, I did not find what I was seeking. So my search continued.

When I came to Oveyssi, the teachings of Hazrat Pir, Molana Salaheddin Ali Nader Shah Angha began to provide the food that had been missing in all other readings, meetings, and intellectual pursuits. Over time I have thrown out many of the concepts and assumptions of prior searchings. There are bound to be many more to fall by the wayside. His teaching and grace allow something real to emerge. Through regular practice and implementation of His teachings things become clear.

I had often deluded myself into thinking I needed to be perfect before I could approach the Master and receive His teachings. However, I, like others, do not possess the power to accomplish this. Only through His teaching can this be done. At times I think otherwise. In spite of how I am thinking, the Master is always there and his Love never varies.

Before meeting Him I evaluated my collection of thoughts and experiences as a treasure. But He showed me that I had nothing but pieces of unworthy glass that shone and reflected some things in some moments that I thought were diamonds. And I was honorably accepted to be taught by His Grace.

All the abilities, powers, capabilities, and talents, inwardly and outwardly, have been granted to mankind by the Ever Alive Existence. What have we done and achieved from all these blessings?

All the endeavors of mankind have been wasted to alter a very small portion of the restricted objects around us, or to invent new facilities for more temporary relief in the natural life. What then is the existential universality of the human being?

Although every point in Existence has a guide line, overwhelmed by the All Universal Power as destiny, humanity is not separate from all the beings. We are living and revolving through eternity and infinity but unaware of the vastness. And it is everlasting.

The *Aref* is the one who graciously wants to show the way and elaborate the talents and educate the inner sources for those who really want to know and recreate and recognize in themselves their own limitless Knowledge that governs, directs, and manifests all beings into this very wonderful manifestation in nature.

Fred Carlsen
Los Angeles, California
September 30, 1988

Fred Carlsen is an electrical engineer and business administrator. For many years he worked in radio in San Francisco. He received his bachelor's and master's degrees from the University of California, Berkeley. He then studied at the Dale Carnegie Institute where he organized studies in human potential. He also studied parapsychology and mysticism at the John F. Kennedy University in California. Throughout his studies, and his activities he sought to find the truth within the holy books, beyond the traditional and ceremonial conceptions of religion. He has been attending classes, seminars and special courses at M.T.O. Shahmaghsoudi (School of Islamic Sufism) for nearly three years.

The Approaching Promise

HE,
THE EXALTED LORD GOD

Through intricate labyrinths revolves
the way to the hidden secrets of heart.

And within His authority lies
the key to this treasure's door.

Should the hand of Him, the treasure's Lord,
open your treasure's door,

To your soul He will reveal
the precious essence of this secret.

HE,
THE EXALTED LORD GOD

Through the four elements —
water, wind, earth and fire —

And on the axis of Four, Five,
Seven, Nine, and Six,

Behold existence's manifestations.
And more magnificent yet,

Should the one revelation illumine your heart,
then keep the vow of silence dear.

Chanteh — Realm of the Aref
By
Our Lord
Molana-al-Moazam Hazrat Shah Maghsoud Sadegh Angha
"Pir Oveyssi"

2

HE,
THE EXALTED LORD GOD

*That fire that sparks the pendulum of time and
   bestows life to the soul,*

*That divine inspiration of Sadegh —
   that savored essence of all spirits,*

*That water of life, that wavy munificence
   imaged into form by the eyes,*

What happened to That? What became of It?

* * *

That witness of the glorious awarenesses
  as infinite as the witnessed,

That seer of feverish hearts
  in the select body and the world,

That worshipper of tenderness —
  that Deity's imparting breath of life,

That lover's kindled heart, absorbed
  by the Beloved's compelling lure,

That reflector of light
  through the prism's wall,

That great unlimited assembly —
  that predicted promise,

That extender of relief to the
  earth-leavened shell and its loads,

That eddy of folded powers, concealed
  within the preserved tablet,

That safeguarded fervent ecstasy —
  that absorbs and revives,

That radiant magnificent star, as a shooting star
  that descends and penetrates,

That pure distilled frenzy of love —
  that creator of Names,

What happened to That? What became of It?

4

That ebullient burgeoning within
the structure of particles,

That bed of ruffled hair imprinted
with the tender breeze of the pure,

That murmur of ever-expanding
waves and heavens,

That morning hubbub of the early riser, arousing
hundred clamours in existence's dome,

That incendiary sigh that harvests with fire
a hundred enraptured suns of love's frenzy,

That silent fermenting of the vein of vine
surging through with drunkenness,

That pure effulgence that sets to glow
the alum and the glass,

That mirror-like treasury of secrets undivulged —
the stable and the bestower,

That nurtured intoxication beheld in
the cup-bearer's cup,

That reviving wave, resurging
from the breeze of dawn,

That beam of justice soaring to
the heavens most high,

What happened to That? What became of It?

That child-like joyfulness, the fervor
    which nourishes the inner self,

That vernal showering rain and
    that lustrous gleaming pearl,

That enshrined beauty wending through
    the mountainous skirts,

That fount of the sun hidden behind
    the darkness of a hundred veils,

That quivering and glittering
    dew of life,

That water drop, flowering to bloom
    the gardens of paradise,

That rejoicing bud which is
    the nightingale's heart,

That lily, that hyacinth,
    that tulip and the foliage,

That blood-straining spring in
    the fields of endearing madness,

That burnt branded heart
    within the tulip's bloom,

That submission of the submitted
    that became wings for the heavens,

What happened to That? What became of It?

That trust which is the honor of virtuous souls,

That entrusted jewel, waywardly
    circling the unknowns,

See how it's flaunted on desires
    of the dust and earth,

Realities became despairing slaves
    covered by their earthenware,

Beds of carcass became the purpose
    for the powers and strengths,

In this cesspool the kite snapped
    away the lily's scent,

Weakness fueled misfortune's strength
    of mud as a mirage,

The flower's throne submerged into
    the swampland of layers — dead,

Strengths into impotence turned and
    tenderness into earthly moulds consumed,

In disappointment of the children of
    greed, slaves to the earth,

A thousand sighs of Adam
    ascended to the dome of existence,

When did it happen? So, it came to be!

* * *

How can I not divulge, this was the
    treasure that was interred.

O soul of souls, my soul was not all you took away,
My heart and belief you pillaged as well.

Your alluring and shining guidance kindles,
The flaming dance of passion and ecstasy so dear.

My portion from your everlasting and inspiring soul I take,
'Til absolute awareness is my enraptured state.

Though, I am enclosed in the coercion of time,
Yet, the resplendent flame of this lantern I am.

Unfold my wings, set me to fly,
From the fortress of these dungeon walls,
*   my liberation grant.*

Nader Angha

Written on the birthday of the lord of the saints,
the king of truth, Ali Morteza (peace be upon him)

Wednesday

13 Rajab	1408
12 Esfand	1366
2 March	1988

به نهان‌خانهٔ دل راه بسی تو در توست

که کلید در این گنج نهان در کف اوست

دست گنجور در گنج تو گر باز کند

با خبر جان تو از گوهر این راز کند

در عنصر آب و باد و خاک و آتش

بر محور چار و پنج و هفت و نه و شش

ترسیم وجود بین و افزون تر از آن

گر یافت دلت نقش دگر دم در کش

چنته (جهان عارف)

اثر مولانا المعظم حضرت شاه مقصود صادق عنقا پیر اویسی

***

آن آتش جان بخش که رقاص زمان است ،

آن نفخهٔ صادق که بود لطف روایح ،

آن آب حیات بذل موّاج که در عین مکان است ،

بکجا رفت ؟   چه ها شد ؟

***

آن شاهد اطوار جلالی بحق وسعت مشهود ،

آن ناظر دلهای تب آلود در این معشر منظور ،

آن عابد الطاف و دم محیی معبود ،

آن عاشق دل سوخته در جذبهٔ معشوق ،

آن ناشر انوار ز دیوارهٔ منشور ،

آن محشر بی حد و کران وعده موعود ،

آن بازگشای صدف خاک و ثقالت ،

آن قدرت ملفوف که مستور به لوح است ،

آن مستی محفوظ که پر جذبه و شور است ،

آن اختر ثاقب که مجلل چو شهاب است ،

آن عشق مروّق ز جنون فاطر اسماء ،

بکجا رفت ؟   چه ها شد ؟

آن رشد درون جوش که درهیئت ذرات ،

آن زلف پریشان ز قدمگاه لطیفان ،

آن زمزمهٔ باسط امواج و سماوات ،

آن غلغلهٔ صبح سحرخیز که صد ولوله در گنبد افلاک بپا کرد ،

آن آه جهانسوز که تلطیف فروزندهٔ صد شمس جنون است ،

آن جوشش خاموش رگ رز که به مستی فیضان داشت ،

آن شعشعهٔ پاک که در زاج و زجاج است ،

آن آینه وش مخزن اسرار که در داد و دهش بود ،

آن مستی پرورده که در ساغر ساقی است ،

آن موج مروّح که نسیم سحری بود ،

آن شاهین عدالت که بود سائر اعلیٔ ،

بکجا رفت ؟   چه ها شد ؟

آن شادی طفلانه وآن شوق درون ساز ،

آن بارش نیسانی وآن دُربدخشان ،

آن حسن دلاویز که بر دامن کهسار روان است ،

آن چشمهٔ خورشید که در ظلمت صد پرده نهان بود ،

آن شبنم لرزان و درخشان حیاتی ،

آن قطره گُل پرور گلزار الستی ،

آن غنچهٔ خندان که بود قلب هَزاران ،

آن سوسن وآن سنبل وآن لاله وریحان ،

آن چشمهٔ خون پالا در دشت جنون بخش ،

آن سوخته در جان شقایق که بود داغ ،

آن سلّموا تسلیم که شد شهپر اسریٰ ،

بکجا رفت ؟   چه ها شد ؟

16

آن امانت که بود عزت ارواح تقی ،

آن مهین گوهر غلطان که نگون سرگشته ،

بین که در خاک و زمین مصرف اهواء گردید ،

حالها شد خادم افسرده ،   مغلوب سفال ،

بستر مردارها شد مقصد توش و توان ،

عطر سوسن را زغن بوئید در این منجلاب ،

ناتوانی قوت ادبار گل شد چون سراب ،

جایگاه گل به مرداب عظیم لایه اندر شد ،

توانها ناتوانی شد ، لطائف بود در این کسوت نابود ،

زناکامی فرزندان حرص و بندگان گل ،

هزار افسوس آدم،   خاست بر سقف سماء ،

کی شد ؟   چه ها شد ؟

***

کتمان چه کنم این را ، گنجی است که مدفون شد.

17

نه همین جان من ای جان بردی

دل و دینم به گروگان بردی

طره تا دام ره ما کردی

فتنه و شور تو بر پا کردی

جرعه نوشم من از آن نرگس مست

که چنین رفته‌ام ای فتنه زدست

منکه در جبر زمان محبوسم

شمع سوزندهٔ این فانوسم

تو به پروازم از این حبس، پران

که شوم رسته از این دام گران

نادرعفا

میلاد ولی اولیاء، سلطان ولا، علی مرتضی (ع)

چهارشنبه ۱۳ رجب ۱۴۰۸

۱۲ اسفند ۱۳۶۶

۲ مارس ۱۹۸۸

La Promesse

AU NOM DE DIEU TOUT PUISSANT

Vers le labyrinthe du cœur,
*   le chemin est tout entremêlé*

Et la clef de ce trésor
*   ′ entre Ses mains se trouve cachée*

Si la main du gardien
*   venait à ouvrir la porte de ton trésor*

Sur l'essence de ce secret,
*   ton âme, il avertirait*

AU NOM DE DIEU TOUT PUISSANT

Parmi les éléments : l'eau, le vent, la terre et le feu

Sur l'axe du Quatre, Cinq, Sept, Neuf et Six

Vois le dessein de l'existence, et plus encore,

Si ton cœur trouve une autre image,

Alors, ne dit plus rien.

Tchanté (L'Univers de Aref)
par
Molana-al-Moazam Hazrat Shah Maghsoud Sadegh Angha
"Pir Oveyssi"

AU NOM DE DIEU TOUT PUISSANT

Ce feu vivifiant, le danseur du temps,

Ce soupir sincère, la grâce des âmes,

Cette eau de vie, générosité ondoyante

Où se mirent toutes les existences

Ou s'en sont-ils allés ? Qu'en est-il advenu ?

* * *

Ce témoin glorieux flamboyant
des vastes espaces visibles,

Ce gardien des cœurs enfiévrés
dans ce dessein d'union,

Ce dévot des grâces,
souffles ressuscitants de l'Adoré,

Cet amoureux chagriné
dans l'attrait du bien-aimé,

Celui qui répand les ondes
rayonnant du mur de réflexions,

Cette résurrection d'horizon infini,
promesse des promesses,

Celui qui soulève la coquille
de poussière et de lourdeur,

Cette puissance voilée,
dissimulée dans les tablettes,

Cette exaltation retenue,
pleine d'attrait et de Passion,

Cette étoile illuminée glorieuse
dans sa grandeur perçante de météore,

Cet amour purifié,
qui de passion créa tous Noms,

Ou s'en sont-ils allés ? Qu'en est-il advenu ?

Ce bouillonnement créateur
    qui agite les particules,

Cette chevelure étalée, emmêlée
    par le passage des tendres,

Ce murmure que déploient
    vagues et firmaments,

Ce bruit de l'Aurore, soufflant
    cent échos sur la voûte céleste,

Ce soupir brûlant, purifiant,
    illuminant des astres de passions,

Ce tumulte calme des veines, de la vigne
    jaillissant en ivresse,

Ce pur étincellement
    des cristaux et des hyalines,

Cette miroitante source de secrets,
    pleine de justice et de grâce,

Ce fruit d'enivrement,
    dans la coupe de la muse,

Cette vague vivifiante,
    la brise de l'aube,

Ce fléau de la balance,
    le voyageur suprême,

Ou s'en sont-ils allés ? Qu'en est-il advenu ?

Cette joie enfantine,
ce désir créateur,

Cette pluie printanière,
ce joyau des plus précieux,

Cette beauté charmante,
coulant au bas des montagnes,

Cette source d'énergie,
dissimulée par cent voiles obscurs,

Cette rosée de l'existence
tremblante et éclatante,

Cette gouttelette d'épanouissement
du jardin de la création,

Ce bouton de fleur souriant,
le cœur des rossignols,

Ce Lis, cette Jacinthe,
cette Tulipe et ces fines herbe,

Cette eau purifiante
dans la plaine enivrante,

Ce coquelicot embrasé dans l'âme,
portant le deuil,

Cette soumission du soumis,
les ailes de l'ascension,

Ou s'en sont-ils allés ? Qu'en est-il advenu ?

Cette offrande, l'honneur des esprits purs,

Ce beau joyau scintillant, de malheur terni,

Regarde-le ! Asservi aux caprices
    dans la poussière et la terre,

Des extases, serviles de mélancolie,
    vaincues par bassesse,

Le lit des morts, devenu le but
    de pouvoir et de richesse,

Parfum du lis, humé par les rapaces
    de ce marécage,

Faiblesse devint la force des malheurs,
    la boue devint mirage,

La demeure des fleurs
    devint l'immense mare de souille,

Les forces devinrent impuissance,
    les grâces se vêtirent de néant,

Par l'échec des enfants de l'avidité,
    esclaves de la chair,

Hélas ! Mille hélas d'Adam
    montèrent vers les cieux.

Quand cela arriva-t-il ? Que s'est-il donc passé ?

* * *

A quoi bon le nier,
    c'est un trésor qui s'est enterré.

27

Mon âme, non seulement tu m'as enlevé l'âme
Tu pris en otage et mon cœur et ma foi

De ta chevelure, comme tu as piégé ma voie
L'instigateur de révolte et d'insurrection, c'est toi

Je bois à la coupe de ce narcisse enivrant
Car tel est mon péril, ô ma sédition, ô mon néant

Emprisonné, par les contraintes du temps
De cette lanterne, je demeure le cierge brûlant

A tire-d'aile Ami, envole-moi de cette prison
Puissé-je être libéré de ce piège pesant

Nader Angha

A l'occasion de l'anniversaire du gardien des gardiens,
le souverain de l'affection et de l'amitié, Ali Morteza,
(La paix soit sur lui)

Mercredi

13 rajab	1408
12 esfand	1366
2 mars	1988

مقترب

(قرب الميعاد)

الطريق إلى أسرار القلب الكمينة يمرّ عبر سبل متشعبة ،
ومفتاح باب هذا الكنز هو عليه مسيطر .

إذا فتحت يد سيّد الكنز باب كنزك ،
ينكشف لك جوهر هذا السرّ العزيز .

هُوَ اللهُ العَلِيّ

الماء والريح ، التراب والنار ،

أربعة وخمسة ، سبعة وتسعة وستّة،

من خلال العناصر والأرقام تأمّل تجلّيات الوجود تزدد في عينيك
روعة ، وإذا نوّر الإلهام قلبك احفظ عهد الصمت الغالي.

عالم العارف

تأليف

سيّدنا ومولانا المعظّم

حضرة الشاه مقصود صادق عنقا

«پير أويسي»

تلك النار التي تضرم رقّاص الزمان وترزق النفس بالحياة ،

ذلك الإلهام الإلٰهي الصادقّي ، ذلك العطر المحبّب لكّل الأرواح ،

ذلك الماء الحيوّي ، ذلك الفيض المتموّج

الذي تعطيه شكله العيون ..

مالذي جرى له ؟ ماذا صار ؟

ذلك الشاهد للوعي المجيد ، مثل المشهود بدون حدود ،

ذلك الذي يبصر القلوب المتأجّجة في العالم وفي الجسد المصطفى،

الذي يعبد اللطف، ذلك النفس الربّانيّ الذي يهب الحياة ،

ذلك القلب المحّب المشتعل المفتون بالمحبوب ،

الذي يعكس النور عبر جدار الموشور البلّوريّ ،

ذلك المحشر الذي لا حدّ له ، تلك النبّوة ، ذلك الوعد ،

الذي يفرّج عن القشرة الأرضيّة المتخمّرة ويخفّف أعباءها ،

تلك الدّوامة من القوى المطوّية الكامنة في اللوح المحفوظ ،

تلك النشوة المضطرمة المصونة التي تجذب وتنعش ،

ذلك النجم المتلألئ الرائع ، كالنيزك ينزل ويتوغّل ،

ذلك الهيجان المقطر الصافي ، هيجان الهوى ، خالق الأسماء..

ما الذي حدث له ؟ ماذا صار ؟

34

ذلك التفتح الجيّاش داخل بنية الأجزاء ،

ذلك السرير من الشعر الهائج المتّسم بنسيم الطاهر الناعم ،

ذلك الهمس من الأمواج والسمٰوات الممتدّة دون انقطاع ،

تلك الضجّة من الصاحي المبكّر ،

مثيرة مئات الضجّات في قبّة الوجود ،

تلك الآهة المضطرمة الحاصدة بالنار

مئة من الشموس الولهانة عشقاً،

ذلك التخمر الصامت لعرق الكرم المتصاعد نشوة ،

ذلك السطوع الطاهر الذي يسبّب توهّج الشّب والزجاج ،

تلك الخزانة ، كمرآة لأسرار مكتومة، ثابتة لا تنقطع عن العطاء،

تلك السكرة التي غذّيت ،

تلك السكرة التي تُبصَر في كأس الساقي،

تلك الموجة المنعشة تصعد ثانية من نسيم الفجر ،

ذلك الشعاع من العدل يرتفع نحو أعلى السمٰوات..

مالذي جرى لذلك ؟ ماذا صار ؟

تلك الغبطة الطفوليّة ، تلك الحرارة التي تغذّي النفس الباطنيّة،

ذلك الغيث الربيعي المنهمر وتلك اللؤلؤة الساطعة المتوهّجة ،

ذلك الحسن المقدّس المصون ، متدلّياً عبر الحواشي المتموّجة ،

ذلك المنهل الشمسيّ ، كامناً وراء ظلمة مئة حجاب ،

ذلك الندى الحيوّي المرتعش المشّع ،

تلك القطرة من الماء المزهرة ، مفتحّة جنان الفردوس ،

ذلك البرعم الفرح ، قلب البلابل ،

تلك السوسنة ، تلك الصّفيرة ، تلك الخزامة والنصال ،

ذلك النبع المطهّر للدماء في مجالات الجنون المعزّ ،

ذلك القلب المكويّ ملتهباً في كمّ الخزامة ،

ذلك الخضوع من المستسلم الذي أضحى أجنحة للسمٰوات ..

ما الذي جرى له ؟ ماذا صار ؟

تلك الثقة ، ذلك الشرف للنفوس الفاضلة ،

تلك الجوهرة ، تلك الأمانة تائهةً في عالم المجهول ،

أنظرْ إليها تهدر على شهوات الأرض والغبار ،

أمست الحقائق سبايا يائسة في طيّ صلصالها ،

أصبحت أسرّة الجثث غاية للقوى والسلطان ،

في هذه الحفرة من الأقذار خطف الطائر الأسود شذى السوسن ،

وزاد وهن مثل السراب من قوّة الخطب في الوحل ،

وانطمس عرش الزهر في طبقات المستنقع ميّتاً ،

فاستحال البأس عجزاً وأُفني اللطف في الرغام .

خيبةً في أطفال الجشع ، عبيد الأرض ،

من آدم ارتفعت ألف آهة نحو قبّة الوجود ..

متى حدث ذلك ؟ ومتى كان ؟

* * *

كيف أملك للسرّ كتماً ، هذا السرّ ذاته الذي دفن .

يا روح الأرواح ، لم تكن روحي كلّ ما أخذته ،
سلبت قلبي وعقيدتي ،

بريق نورك الجذّاب يشعل
رقصة الوجد الملتهبة والنشوة العزيزة .

حصّتي من روحك ذات الخلود والإلهام آخذها ،
إلى أن يصبح الوعي المطلق حالة ولهي .

ولئن قهرت في أسر الزمن
فإنّني الآن لهيب هذا القنديل الوهّاج .

فاطلق جناحّي ، دعني أطير
من قلعة جدران هذا الديماس ،
أعطني حرّيّتي .

نادر عنقا

كتب في عيد ميلاد سيّد الأولياء ،
ملك الحقّ ، عليّ مرتضى (عليه السلام)
يوم الأربعاء ١٣ رجب ١٤٠٨
١٢ اسفند ١٣٦٦
٢ مارس ١٩٨٨

L'Avvicinarsi Della Promessa

EGLI, L'ESALTATO SIGNORE DIO

Attraverso intricati labirinti rotea
    il sentiero ai nascosti segreti del cuore.

Ed entro la Sua autorità giace,
    la chiave alla porta di questo tesoro.

Dovrebbe la mano di Lui, il tesoro del Signore,
    aprire la porta del tuo tesoro,

Al tuo spirito, Egli rivelerà
    la preziosa essenza di questo segreto.

EGLI, L'ESALTATO SIGNORE DIO

Attraverso i quattro elememti —
acqua, vento, terra e fuoco —

E sull'asse di Quattro, Cinque,
Sette, Nove, e Sei,

Mirate le manifestazioni dell'esistenza.
E ancora piú magnifico

Dovrebbe quella rivelazione illuminare il tuo cuore,
poi tenere cara la promessa del silenzio.

Chanteh-Reame dell'Aref
del
Nostro Signore
Molana-al-Moazam Hazrat Shah Maghsoud Sadegh Angha
"Pir Oveyssi"

EGLI, L'ESALTATO SIGNORE DIO

Quel fuoco che scintilla il pendolo del tempo e
   dona vita allo spirito,

Quella divina ispirazione di Sadegh —
   quella saporita essenza di tutti gli spiriti,

Quell'acqua di vita, quella ondosa munificenza
   ritrattata in una forma dagli occhi,

Che accadde a Quello? Che Divenne di Esso?

* * *

Quel testimone della gloriosa consapevolezza
  infinito quanto il testimoniato,

Quel veggente di cuori febbrili
  nel corpo scelto ed il mondo,

Quell'adoratore di tenerezza — quella divinità
  che distribuisce respiro di vita,

Quell'amante dal cuore acceso, assorbito
  dall'obbligato fascino dell'amato,

Quel riflettore di luce,
  attraverso il muro del prisma,

Quella grande illimitata assemblea
  che predisse promessa,

Quel prolungatore di sollievo alla conchiglia
  formata da terra ed il suo carico,

Quelle numerose piegate potenze, celate
  entro conservata tavoletta,

Quella salvaguardata fervente estasi,
  che concentra e ravviva,

Quella radiante magnifica stella, come
  una stella filante che discende e penetra,

Quella pura distillata frenesia d'amore —
  quel creatore di Nomi,

Che accadde a Quello? Che avenne di Esso?

Quel bollente germogliare entro
    la struttura delle cellule,

Quella superficie di increspati capelli fissati
    con la tenera brezza del puro,

Quel mormorio di onde e cieli, sempre
    in espansione

Quello schiamazzo del mattino della persona mattutina
    svegliando cento clamori nel duomo dell'esistenza

Quell'incendario sospiro che raccoglie con fuoco
    un centinàio di soli incantati dalla
    frenesia dell'amore,

    Quel silenzioso fermento della vena di vite
        insorgente con ubbriachezza,

    Quel puro lustro che inizia ad ardere
        l'allume ed il vetro,

    Quella tesoreria come specchio di celati segreti
        lo stabile ed il donatore,

    Quella nutrita intossicazione ammirata nella
        tazza del portatore della tazza,

    Quella ravvivante onda, risorgente
        dalla brezza dell'aurora,

    Quel raggio di giustizia ascendendo
        ai cieli piu alti,

    Che accadde a Quello? Che divenne di Esso?

Quella allegrezza da bambino, il fervore
   che nutrisce l'interno di stesso,

Quel primaverile scrosciare della pioggia e
   quella lucente brillante perla,

Quella conservata santa bellezza proseguendo
   attraverso gli orli delle montagne,

Quella fonte del sole nascosta dietro
   l'oscurità di cento veli,

Quel tremito e lucente rugiada
   di vita,

Quella goccia d'acqua, fiorita a infiorare
   i giardini del paradiso,

Quel gioioso germoglio, il quale è
   l'usignolo del cuore

Quel giglio, quel giacinto,
   quel tulipano ed il fogliame,

Quel sangue filtrando primavera nei
   campi di affettuosa follia,

Quel bruciato marchiato cuore
   entro il fiorente tulipano,

Quella sottomissione del sottomesso
   che divenne ali per i cieli,

Che accadde a Quello? Che divenne di Esso?

Quella fiducia che è l'onore
 degli spiriti virtuosi,

Quell affidata gioia,
 capriccisamente accerchiando gli sconosciuti,

Guarda come essa è sfoggiata di
 desideri della polvere e terra,

Realtà divennero disperati schiavi
 coperti dal loro terraglio,

Aiuole di carcame divennero il proposito
 per i poteri e le forze,

In questa fogna il profumo del giglio
 è esteso dappertutto,

La debolezza alimentò la forza delle
 sfortuna del fango come un mizeggio

Il trono del fiore sommerse dentro
 la paludosa terra di veli-morta,

Forze tornarono alla impotenza e
 tenerezza si consumò nei terricci mondani,

In disappunto dei figli della
 avidità schiavi della terra,

Un migliaio di sospiri di Adamo
 ascesero al duomo dell'esistenza,

Quando esso accadde? Cosí, Esso divenne Essere?

* * *

Come posso non divulgere, questo era il
 tesoro che era seppellito.

O spirito di spiriti, il mio spirito non era tutto
    quello che tu portasti via,
Mio cuore e fede tu anche saccheggiasti.

La tua affascinante e brillante guida accende,
La fiammante danza di passione ed estasi cosi cara.

La mia porzione dal tuo eterno ed ispirato spirito
    Io prendo,
Finché assoluta consapevolezza è il mio incantato stato.

Benché, sono rinchiuso nella coartazione del tempo,
Tuttavia, la rieplendente fiamma
    di questa laterna Io sono.

Slega le mie ali, fammi volare,
Dalla fortezza di queste sotterranee mura,
    la mia liberazione concedi.

Nader Angha

Scritto al compleanno del signore dei santi, il re della
verità, Ali Morteza (pace sia su di lui)

Mercoledí

13 Rajab	1408
12 Esfand	1366
2 Marzo	1988

La Promesa Se Aproxima

ÉL,
EL DIOS ALTÍSIMO

Por los intrincados laberintos del corazón
serpea el sendero hacia sus recónditos secretos.

Y en sus manos tiene
la llave del tesoro.

Si la mano de tu Señor
abriese la puerta de tu tesoro,

Le revelaría a tu alma
la preciosa esencia de dicho secreto.

ÉL,
EL DIOS ALTÍSIMO

Entre los cuatro elementos:
agua, viento, tierra y fuego

Y sobre el eje de cuatro, cinco,
siete, nueve y seis

Contempla las manifestaciones de la existencia.
Y si en su esplendor,

Una revelación te iluminase el corazón
no rompas el silencio.

Cántico — El Universo de Aref
por
Molana-al-Moazam Hazrat Shah Maghsoud Sadegh Angha
"Pir Oveyssi"

ÉL,
EL DIOS ALTÍSIMO

Aquella llama que enciende el péndulo del tiempo
e imprime vida al alma,

Aquella divina inspiración de Sadegh
esencia sabrosísima de todo espíritu,

Aquel agua vivificante, aquella generosidad ondulante
a la que los ojos dan forma,

¿Dónde está? ¿Qué le ha ocurrido?

*   *   *

Aquel testigo resplandeciente y glorioso
  de los vastos espacios visibles,

Aquél que ve los corazones febriles
  palpitando en este mundo,

Aquél que adora la ternura
  aquella Divinidad que exhala el aliento de vida,

Aquel ardiente corazón de Amante absorto
  por el irresistible encanto del Amado,

Aquel reflejo de luz
  en la pared del prisma,

Aquella immensa asamblea —
  promesa de promesas,

Aquél que alivia el cuerpo
  de la costra de polvo y la fatiga,

Aquella potencia de poderes,
  impresos en las tablas conservadas,

Aquella exaltación discreta
  plena de atracción y de pasión,

Aquella gloriosa estrella iluminada
  con su grandiosa penetración meteórica,

Aquel amor purificante
  cuya pasión crea todos los Nombres,

¿Dónde está? ¿Qué le ha ocurrido?

Aquel exuberante retoñar dentro
    de la estructura de los átomos,

Aquella onda de encrispados cabellos
    estampada con la tierna brisa de lo puro,

Aquel susurro de ondas y cielos
    siempre en expansión,

Aquel grito del que madruga
    levantando clamores en la bóveda de la existencia,

Aquel suspiro candente que torna
    el frenesí del amor en soles que extasían,

Aquella fermentación muda de la vid
    que brota embriagada de la viña,

Aquella pura incandescencia
    que hace resplandecer al alumbre y al cristal,

Aquel tesoro, espejo de callados secretos
    lo estable y lo otorgado,

Aquella intoxicación tan delicadamente cuidada
    en la copa del portado de la copa,

Aquella ola vivificadora, resurgiendo
    de la brisa del alba,

Aquel haz de justicia ascendiendo
    a lo más alto de los cielos,

¿Dónde está? ¿Qué le ha ocurrido?

*Aquel regocijo infantil, el fervor
que nutre lo más íntimo,*

*Aquella lluvia de primavera y
la reluciente y brillante perla,*

*Aquella consagrada belleza siguiendo
la falda de la montaña,*

*Aquella fontana de sol oculta tras
la sombra de cien velos,*

*Aquel palpitante y luciente
rocío de vida,*

*Aquella gota de agua iluminando el florecer de
los jardines del paraíso,*

*Aquel alegre capullo
corazón del ruiseñor,*

*Aquel lirio, ese jacinto
el tulipán y el follaje,*

*Aquella sangre filtrando primaveras
sobre los campos de afectuosa demencia,*

*Aquel corazón sellado al fuego
entre tulipanes en flor,*

*Aquella sumisión del sometido
tornada en alas celestiales,*

¿Dónde está? ¿Qué le ha ocurrido?

Aquel confiar, honor de espíritus virtuosos,

Aquella alhaja que se te ha confiado,
circulando caprichosamente lo ignorado,

Observa como ostenta
polvorientos deseos mundanos,

Realidades reducidas a esclavitud desesperada,
cubiertas de barro,

Poderes y potencias se pusieron al servicio
de lo que estaba muerto,

Y en esa sentina el cuervo le arrancó
su perfume al lirio,

La debilidad alimentó la fuerza del infortunio
del lodo como un espejismo,

El trono de las flores sumergido
yace en capas de lodazal — muerto,

La fortaleza transformada en impotencia y
la ternura consumida en moldes de lodo,

Viendo el trágico estado de los hijos de
la codicia, esclavos de la tierra,

Adán deja escapar mil suspiros
que ascienden hasta la bóveda de la existencia.

¿Cuándo sucedió? ¡Así acaeció!

* * *

Y cómo no he de divulgarlo si ese
era el tesoro enterrado.

Oh alma de almas, no sólo me arrebataste el alma,
Sino que también te has llevado mi corazón y mi fe.

Tu seductora y luminosa pauta enciende
La cálida danza de pasión y éxtasis.

Tomo mi parte de tu alma sempiterna e inspiradora,
Hasta que mi ser se empape de certeza absoluta.

Aunque preso en el plano del tiempo humano esté,
Soy la llama refulgente de ese faro.

Despliega mis alas, lánzame al vuelo,
Y de esta amurallada prisión
*   concédeme la liberación.*

Nader Angha

Escrito en el cumpleaños del señor de los santos,
el rey de la verdad, Ali Morteza
(la paz sea con él)

Miércoles

13 Radjab	1408
12 Esfand	1366
2 de marzo	1988

Die Nahende Verheißung

ER, DER ALLMÄCHTIGE GOTT

Durch verschlungene Pfade führt
  der Weg zur geheimsten Herzenskammer,

Und in Seiner Hand allein
  liegt der Schlüssel zum Schatz.

Wenn Er, der Schatzeshüter, kommt,
  Deine Geheimtür zu öffnen —

Deiner Seele wird er enthüllen
  des Geheimnis' kostbarste Perle.[1]

ER, DER ALLMÄCHTIGE GOTT

Durch die vier Elemente
    Wasser, Wind, Erde und Feuer,

Und auf den Achsen Vier, Fünf,
    Sieben, Neun und Sechs,

Betrachte den Schöpfungsplan
    und Großartiges mehr —

Entzündet die eine Offenbarung Dein Herz,
    dann halte das Versprechen des Schweigens.

Tschante — Die Welt eines Sufi
ein Werk von
Molana-al-Moazam Hazrat Shah Maghsoud Sadegh Angha
"Pir Oveyssi"

ER, DER ALLMÄCHTIGE GOTT

Das Feuer, das das Rad der Zeit bewegt
und der Seele Leben gibt,

Dieser göttliche Hauch von Sadegh,[2]
der kostbarste aller Düfte,

Dies Wasser des Lebens, diese wallende Großzügigkeit
formt der Blick zum Bild.

Was geschah damit? Was ist daraus geworden?

* * *

Dies Zeugnis glorreicher Erkenntnis
so unendlich wie das Enthüllte,

Dieser Hüter des fiebernden Herzens,
in erwählter Gestalt, in der Welt,

Dieser Priester der Sanftmut —
göttlicher Atem des Lebens,

Des Liebenden entfachtes Herz, gefangen
durch des Geliebten zwingendes Verlangen,

Des Lichtes Widerschein
durch die Spiegelwand,

Das Ende der Endlichkeit,
die verkündete Verheißung,

Der allumfassende Erlöser
der erdverhafteten Hülle und ihrer Lasten,

Der Wirbel verhaltener Kräfte,
verborgen in der geschützten Tafel,

Die Leidenschaft, bewacht, verzückt,
die nimmt und wiedergibt,

Der Stern, der prächtig strahlt
sternschnuppengleich erleuchtet und erlischt,

Der innigste Taumel der Liebe,
der alles benennt,

Was geschah damit? Was ist daraus geworden?

Der treibende Sproß, vollkommen,
inmitten jedes Seins,

Der Lockenschopf,
in dem der zarte Hauch des Reinen liegt,

Das Raunen ewig wachsender
Wellen und Himmel,

Der Tumult des Morgengrauens —
hundertfach hallt sein Echo im Himmelsgewölbe,

Der brennende Seufzer, der die Sonne der Liebe
aufhellt und entflammt,

Das pulsierende Gären in den Adern des Weinstocks,
das mit Trunkenheit erfüllt,

Das helle Funkeln
der Gläser und Kristalle,

Der spiegelnde Quell der Geheimnisse,
voller Gerechtigkeit und Gnade,

Der reifende Rausch,
der im Becher des Mundschenks liegt,

Die erweckende Woge
der Morgendämmerung,

Das Kreuz der Gerechtigkeit,
das zum höchsten Himmel ragt,

Was geschah damit? Was ist daraus geworden?

Die kindliche Freude, Leidenschaft
und Mahnung des inneren Selbst,

Der Frühlingsschauer
und die schimmernde, funkelnde Perle,

Die ewig vollkommene Schönheit —
Farbenglanz am Fuß der Berge,

Der Brunnen der Lebenskraft
versteckt hinter hundert Schleiern,

Der perlende, glitzernde
Lebenstau,

Der Tropfen,
der das Paradies erblühen läßt,

Der Blume lächelnde Knospe,
der Nachtigallen Herz,

Die Lilie, die Hyazinthe,
die Tulpe und jungsprießendes Laub,

Der reinigende Quell
in der Wüste des lockenden Wahnsinns,

Das Brandmal im Herzen
der Tulpenblüte,

Die Ergebenheit des Ergebenen
mit den Schwingen zur Himmelsfahrt,

Was geschah damit? Was ist daraus geworden?

Der Glaube,
 der die Ehre der tugendhaften Seelen ist,

Das Juwel, geheimnisvoll funkelnd,
 doch den Unglücklichen blind,

Sieh, wie es sich gemeinen Launen
 beugen mußte in Erde und Staub,

Überschwang wurde zum Diener des Trübsinns,
 besiegt durch Erbärmlichkeit,

Totenbetten wurden zum Ziel
 von Kraft und Vermögen,

In diesem Sumpf roch auch der Geier
 nur noch der welkenden Lilien Duft,

Schwäche treibt einzig die Kraft des
 schmutzigen Unheils an,

Der Thron der Blume versinkt
 in den Tiefen des Sumpfes — tot

Kraft wurde Schwäche,
 die Zartheit hüllt sich in weltlichen Staub.

Aus Enttäuschung über die Habgier der Kinder,
 der erdverhafteten Sklaven,

steigen tausend Seufzer Adams
 zum Himmelszelt.

Wann ist das geschehen? Wie konnte das passieren?

* * *

Wie kann ich das verschweigen,
 es war der Schatz, der vergraben wurde.

Oh, Seele der Seelen, nicht nur meine Seele hast Du mir
geraubt, auch Herz und Glauben plündertest Du,

Dein lockendes, leuchtendes Leitbild entfacht
den flammenden Tanz von Versuchung und Eifer.

Meinen Trunk nehme ich aus Deinem Brunnen der
Versuchung, denn dies ist mein Schicksal
bis zur wahren Erkenntnis.

Die Zeit hält mich gefangen,
die ausbrennende Kerze dieser Laterne bin ich.

Lass' Wind aufziehen und lass' mich fliegen
aus diesen Kerkermauern — gib mir die Freiheit!

Nader Angha

Am Geburtstag des Koenigs der Heiligen, Ali'je Morteza
(Er sei gegrüßt)

Mittwoch

13 Rajab	1408
12 Esfand	1366
2 Maerz	1988

ERKLÄRUNGEN

1. *Die Perle ist die wörtliche Übersetzung des Ausdruckes "Gohar". Mit diesem Ausdruck meinen viele Sufis "die göttlichen Eigenschaften".*

2. *Wörtlich bedeutet es "aufrichtig", "wahrhaftig". Es ist auch der Vorname von Molana-al-Moazam Hazrat Shah Maghsoud Sadegh Angha, "Pir Oveyssi."*

Genealogy of the School of Islamic Sufism
Maktab Tarighe Oveyssi Shahmaghsoudi

Prophet Mohammad
Imam Ali

1. Hazrat Oveys Gharani
2. Hazrat Salman Farsi
3. Hazrat Abu Salim Habib-ibn Moussa Zeyd Rai
4. Hazrat Soltan Ebrahim Adham
5. Hazrat Abu Ali Shaghigh Balkhi
6. Hazrat Sheikh Abu Torab Nakhshabi
7. Hazrat Sheikh Abi Amr Estakhri
8. Hazrat Abu Ja'far Hazza
9. Hazrat Sheikh Kabir Abu Abdollah Mohammad-ibn Khafif Shirazi
10. Hazrat Sheikh Hossein Akkar
11. Hazrat Sheikh Morshed Abu-Eshagh Shahriar Kazerouni
12. Hazrat Khatib Abolfath Abolghassem Abdolkarim
13. Hazrat Ali-ibn Hassan Salebeh Basri
14. Hazrat Serajeddin Abolfath Mahmoud-ibn Mahmoudi Sabouni Beyzavi
15. Hazrat Sheikh Abu Abdollah Rouzbehan Baghli Shirazi
16. Hazrat Sheikh Najmeddin Tamat-al Kobra Khivaghi
17. Hazrat Sheikh Ali Lala Ghaznavi
18. Hazrat Sheikh Ahmad Zaker Jowzeghani
19. Hazrat Noureddin Abdolrahman Esfarayeni
20. Hazrat Sheikh Rokneddin Alaodowleh Semnani
21. Hazrat Mahmoud Mazdaghani
22. Hazrat Amir Seyyed Ali Hamedani
23. Hazrat Sheikh Ahmad Khatlani
24. Hazrat Seyyed Mohammad Abdollah Ghatifi-al Hassavi Nourbakhsh
25. Hazrat Shah Ghassem Feyzbakhsh
26. Hazrat Hossein Abarghoui Janbakhsh
27. Hazrat Darvish Malek Ali Joveyni
28. Hazrat Darvish Ali Sodeyri
29. Hazrat Darvish Kamaleddin Sodeyri
30. Hazrat Darvish Mohammad Mozaheb Karandehi
31. Hazrat Mir Mohammad Moemen Sodeyri Sabzevari
32. Hazrat Mir Mohammad Taghi Shahi Sabzevari
33. Hazrat Mir Mozafar Ali Shahi
34. Hazrat Mir Mohammad Ali
35. Hazrat Seyyed Shamseddin Mohammad
36. Hazrat Seyyed Abdolvahab Naini
37. Hazrat Haj Mohammad Hassan Kouzekanani
38. Hazrat Agha Abdolghader Jahromi
39. Hazrat Jalaleddin Ali Mir Abolfazl Angha
40. Hazrat Mir Ghotbeddin Mohammad Angha
41. Hazrat Shah Maghsoud Sadegh Angha
42. Hazrat Salaheddin Ali Nader Shah Angha